SUCCESS WORDS FOR SUCCESS

A. J. ROLLS

Order this book online at www.trafford.com
or email orders@trafford.com

Most Trafford titles are also available at major online book retailers.

© Copyright 2019 A. J. Rolls.

All rights reserved. No part of this publication may be reproduced, stored in a retrieval system, or transmitted, in any form or by any means, electronic, mechanical, photocopying, recording, or otherwise, without the written prior permission of the author.

Print information available on the last page.

ISBN: 978-1-4907-9264-4 (sc)
ISBN: 978-1-4907-9263-7 (e)

Because of the dynamic nature of the Internet, any web addresses or links contained in this book may have changed since publication and may no longer be valid. The views expressed in this work are solely those of the author and do not necessarily reflect the views of the publisher, and the publisher hereby disclaims any responsibility for them.

Any people depicted in stock imagery provided by Getty Images are models, and such images are being used for illustrative purposes only.
Certain stock imagery © Getty Images.

Trafford rev. 04/25/2019

 www.trafford.com

North America & international
toll-free: 1 888 232 4444 (USA & Canada)
fax: 812 355 4082

CONTENTS

CHAPTER TITLE	PAGE

Dedication vii

Foreword ix

1   Success Words For Success 1
2   World of Words 15
3   Your Words Are You 23
4   Program Yourself with Success Words 29
5   The Magic of Words 37
6   I Am The Words I Say 41
7   God is My Words 45
8   Command Your Words 49
9   My Words Are My Life 55
10 Magic Atomic Words 59
11 19th Power Words 71
12 Paint A Picture With Your Words 77
13 I Am That I Am Are The Words I Use 85
14 I Know You By The Words You Say 91
15 13 is A Lucky Number 97

Summary & Conclusion 103

Author's Bio 113

Products Available 117

DEDICATION

To President Barack Obama, First Lady Michelle Obama and the First Children.

President Obama please accept this small token of my appreciation for your ability to command the English language to release the positive attributes within the power of words.

Your words once released from you seemingly activate a positive atomic chain reaction into the atmosphere that effect people of all race, color, age, and social economical group, and have a positive affect on them.

Your words resonate within the human soul and spirit, which elicits trust, faith, hope, unity and purpose amongst the inhabitants of planet Earth.

The proof is in your results. You are trusted, loved and appreciated all over planet earth. Thank you President Dr. Barack H. Obama for your sacrifices you made for all of us.

FOREWORD

Each day the words you choose are breaking or making you. Yes there are different languages with different words. The unique part about different languages having different words is that each word has meaning.

Each word comes with its own soul. The soul provides life.

Each word has its own spiritual energy.

Each word has its own emotions.

Each word draws a mental picture.

Each word physically affects us.

Each word ignites the laws of cause and effect throughout the seen and unseen realm.

Your words are a major part of your life. This book success words will help you help yourself use the best possible words in your life time journey.

CHAPTER 1

SUCCESS WORDS FOR SUCCESS

If you take the time to use the success words associated with what you want, you will take the time to do the work to get the success results you want.

If you don't take the time to use the success words of what you want, you won't take the time to do the work to get the success results you want.

WORDS FOR SUCCESS

- You are the words you say.//
- You are the words you think.
- You are the words you feel.
- You paint a picture with your words.
- Your life is the words you use.

SUCCESS WORDS FOR SUCCESS

From the time you are born, until the day you die.

Your words are a major part of your life and influence you.

- As a baby, words develop you.
- As a young adult, words influence you.
- As a senior citizen, your words are you.

The words you hear, the words you read, the words you watch on TV, the words you hear through radio, the words you hear from other people, the words on billboards are all developing & programming you or have developed and programmed some aspect of you.

That is why it is important you never go to sleep watching TV or listening to the radio, unless what you are watching on TV or listening to on the radio:

- Will resurrect you.
- Will encourage you.
- Will Inspire you.
- Will motivate you.
- Will help you help yourself.

When you go to sleep whatever words your conscious mind hear while you're sleeping will seep into your subconscious mind and influence you. In other words you will be programed from the words you hear to:

- Feel like the word or words.
- Act like the words.
- Function like the words.
- Be like the words.

Consciously we are the gate keeper as to what words we accept or reject.

Your conscious mind can differentiate between truth & fiction.

Your subconscious mind is highly impressionable in that it does not differentiate between the truth or a lie.

While you are sleep and your TV or radio is on, your subconscious mind or still playing, where in you can hear the words. Those words are passing through your conscious mind and going straight to your subconscious mind as the truth.

That is why some parents do not let their children watch horror movies before going to sleep in that their conscious mind will adapt that story as a part of their life and play it for them in their subconscious mind when they go to sleep at night.

This book is not about the conscious, subconscious or divine mind. This book about success words. Words have an automatic functioning in your life without your conscious effort.

- You do not consciously make your heart beat.
- You do not consciously make yourself breathe even when you are sleep at night.
- You do not consciously keep yourself from falling out your bed when you go to sleep at night.
- You did not consciously develop yourself in your mother's womb.
- You do not consciously heal yourself when you are hurt.
- You do not consciously control your digestive system.
- You do not consciously keep your heart beating and blood regulating in your body.
- You do not consciously regulate your blood pressure.

Your automatic system is controlled by your subconscious mind. Your subconscious mind regulates, guides, instructs, directs and maintains all these functions of your body without your conscious effort.

Whatever you feed your subconscious mind or allow your conscious mind to feed your subconscious mind is the effect you will get,

SUCCESS WORDS FOR SUCCESS

Good or bad True or false
Negative or positive Right or wrong
Helpful or hurtful Now or later

You can program your subconscious mind through:

- Success Resurrection
- Thoughts
- Feelings
- Repetition
- Prayer
- Visualizing
- Auto suggestion
- Self Hypnosis
- Self talk
- 19th Power
- Consistency
- Declarations
- Affirmations
- Hypnosis
- Subliminal Programming
- Success Words
- Inspiration
- Positive Thinking
- Church
- Sermons
- Cd's
- Internal/External Development

The most powerful and effective programming technique for subconscious programming is simple words.

- Words give life to rejuvenate your soul.
- Words paint a picture in your mind.
- Words elicit an emotion in your emotions.
- Words provide a spiritual energy.
- Words energize your body to action.
- Words get the attention and ear of God.

The top line is everything uses words to describe itself.

- Words have meaning.
- Words have power.
- Words are atomic.
- Atomic words attribute to change.

Because atomic nuclear words have the same chain reaction as with a nuclear blast. Once an atom is released in a nuclear warhead it multiplies itself and in turn increases its impact. Albert Einstein was instrumental in releasing the power of and within the atom. Once the power of the atom is released there is a ripple, duplicating, effect that destroys anything within its area of impact. Miles away from impact of release release words effect can be felt from where the word is released and the effects of the word (Cause) can make an impact miles away.

Once you release a word into the atmosphere, this word will:

- Cause an effect.
- Build momentum.
- Increase in its power.
- Build or tear down.
- Impact its immediate area of release and areas far away depending on the vehicle the word uses to deliver its meaning. The vehicle could and can be:

- Newspaper
- Lecture
- Movie
- Radio
- Book
- Billboard
- Speech
- Magazine
- TV

The release of a word as in the release of an atom will have a cause and effect impact.

Albert Einstein released the power of the atom to create atomic nuclear power. When you release a word you are releasing atomic power within the world to exact a change. In that the power of atomic power releases the power of change.

You have an option as to what direction you are giving the power of your atomic power words.

Your words can:

Build or destroy	Uplift or tear down
Help or hurt	Create or destruct
Unite or separate	Make happy or make sad
Encourage or discourage	Unite or tear apart

Your words effect your invisible and non tangible realm which elicits visible and physical realm changes.

Examples of your invisible and non tangible realm, effecting your visible and tangible realm are:

- Success Resurrection
- Meditation
- Visualization
- Prayer
- Affirmations
- Declarations
- Auto suggestion

- Subliminal Programming
- Hypnotism
- Motivation
- Inspiration
- Positive Thinking
- 19th Power
- Be A Millionaire Now
- Be A Billionaire Now

Each of the preceding areas have a nonphysical invisible origin that derive a physical effect that gets a physical change, experienced as physical manifestation.

Every word you use, has an effect on your life.

Cause and Effect:

If you punch a person in the face (cause) you will get a response (effect). Your effect may be:

- You are hit.
- Law Suit.
- Fine.
- Arrested.

Cause and Effect:

If you walk up to a person and give them, $100.00 dollars (cause). The person's response (effect) will probably be:

- Thank you.
- They like you.
- They show friendship.
- They smile at you.
- They feel good about you.

Your words are the same as a punch to a person's face or giving a person $100.00 to keep. You will get an effect.

SUCCESS WORDS FOR SUCCESS

All of your words have a cause and effect.

Your words have the power to heal, make well, build, resurrect, create, repair, prosper, increase, love & help.

Words are the key to activate & access the power of prayer.

Words enable you to communicate with God, remove evil from your soul, recharge your spirit, control your emotions, strengthen your mind & command your physical body, your money, your marriage, and career.

Once you have established a word, you have given the word a life. Define the word and understand the definition you have given the word. The picture you have of the word. The emotion you feel from the word. The spiritual energy the word gives you. When you use the word that is the effect you will get and live. You gave the word a soul life, solar energy.

Your words will influence your:

- Personality
- Character
- Self image
- Confidence
- Self Esteem
- Energy
- Money
- Career
- Business
- Performance
- Family
- Friends
- Situations
- Opportunities
- Love
- Health
- Happiness
- Success
- Prosperity
- Life Style

Your words will attempt and magnetize to you the words you use.

Your words will express themselves as a word picture in your mind. The picture can be:

- Success or failure
- Prosperous or poverty
- Rich or poor
- Healthy or sickly
- Desirable or undesirable

- Millionaire or broke
- Billionaire or Welfare

Once you have the word picture in your mind, your physical environment will develop that picture in your physical life. Your physical life will be a picture that originated in your:

Soul, Spirit, Emotions, and Mind.

Why?

The atomic words you focus on within you in your invisible and non tangible realm will develop on the outside of you as, visible and tangible.

Youthfulness	Health	People
Love	Happiness	Places
Things	Money	Love

There are various ways a word can get in you. Words can get in you by:

- Saying the word.
- Thinking the word.
- Reading the word.
- Listening to the word.
- Observing the word.
- Feeling the word.
- Looking at the word.

The words you read will help you or hurt you.

The words you hear can program your subconscious mind if heard enough times or repeated by you.

The words you allow yourself to feel will determine your happiness, contentment, joy, or peace.

SUCCESS WORDS FOR SUCCESS

When you look at a word you will elicit a picture in your mind.

- Whatever you're around has words to describe it. These words will affect you for good or bad.

How do you live the words of who you are?

I have developed a program called 19th power.

19th Power is an auto suggestion, self hypnosis, subliminal program that will counteract the counterproductive words you are subjected to each day, and increase within you the power of certain words.

This is not about me selling you anything; this is about helping you to help yourself, through and from atomic words.

Other ways of counteracting counterproductive words are:

- Church
- Gospel radio stations
- Avoid:
    Toxic People, toxic places and toxic things.
- Success Resurrection
- Mediation of what and who you truly are.
- Self talk
- Affirmations
- Declarations

If you are subjected to a negative word, first confront the word attributing to the feeling, thought, or memory, you are experiencing.

Tell the unwanted word. Word I hear you, but this word is not what I am. This word is not who I am. This is the word that I am, (say the word). This is the word of who I am, (say the word).

Tell the word you do not want. Word, I am now deleting this word out of my life. Give the word you do not want a funeral. The best way to do this is provided to you in my CD Titled, Success Resurrector.

Success Resurrector CD will provide you a supernatural deliverance in your life.

Once again this is not about me selling a CD to you. My objective is to provide you maximum impact to have the maximum result you want.

CHAPTER 2

WORLD OF WORDS

What words do you want to:

- Experience in your life?

- Experience on the inside of you?

- Experience on the outside of you?

World of Words.

The world of words have two universes. One on the outside of you and one on the inside of you. Whatever words you:

- Use on the inside of you.
- Think on the inside of you.
- Say on the inside of you.
- Repeat on the inside of you.
- Feel on the inside of you.
- Believe as true on the inside of you.
- Accept on the inside of you.
- Picture on the inside of you.
- Hear on the inside of you.

Attribute to the following:

1. Program certain instructions and directions on the inside you that you experience on the outside of you.

2. Attribute to your self image.

3. Attribute to your self confidence.

4. Attribute to your self esteem.

5. Attribute to your charisma.

The words you live, on the inside of you. Determine what you are, who you are, how you are, what you do, how you live, what you achieve, how successful you are, how prosperous you are, what you have, how much you are worth, your income; and your position in life.

Take for example the cause and effect of certain words.

If you use these cause words what do you think the effect will be?

Words that are positive:

- Uplifting words
- Positive words
- Encouraging words
- Life giving words
- Optimistic words
- Strong positive words
- Motivating words
- Inspirational words

Words that are negative:

Words that are depressing.
Words that are pessimistic.
Words that are negative.
Words that are sad.
Words that are mad.
Words that are destructive.
Words that are hateful.
Words that are weak.

Positive Words like:

Up	Yes	Forgive
Peace	First	Cando
Happy	Joy	Forward
Love	Plenty	Achieve
Win	Surplus	Succeed
Success	Prosperity	

Negative Words like:

Can't	Loss	Impossible
No	Hate	Back
Lack	Down	Lose
Lost	Backward	Limit
Less	Shortage	Can't
Evil	Won't	Impossible

Your words on the inside (internally) of you effect the outside of you.

The words you experience on the outside (externally) of you, effect the inside of you:

You experience these words from various vehicles that transport and deliver words to you.

Word vehicles like:

Conversations   Internet

SUCCESS WORDS FOR SUCCESS

If a word attempts to hijack you do not give into this **(((weed)))** word. If the word is not you, or not what you want, it is a weed word.

If you do not want the weed word in your life, do not give in to the weed word.

Always remind yourself of what words you are not and what words you are.

I have developed a very effective auto suggestion, self hypnosis, subliminal program for you to counteract the words that attempt to have life in you through your soul, spirit, emotions, mind and physical environment. This program is called:

19th Power
19th Power consist of:

1. One book
2. One CD
3. 19 Posters

I have founded and created 19th Power.com. 19th Power.com objective and purpose is to help you help yourself.

As a child you are influenced by the following word vehicles that transport words to you.

Father	Children	School Teacher
Mother	Babysitter	Siblings
Day Care	Friends	Sports

As a teenager your areas expand wherein you receive your words. Through:

Home	Environment	Work
Parents	Music	Classes
Teenagers	School	Slang
College	Church	Friends

As an adult your environment is unlimited. As an adult your life is based on words.

Now that you know, you are responsible for the words you use, the words you use are what you are, what you have, what you achieve, what you magnetize and attract to you.

- Prayers are words
- Affirmations are words
- Declarations are words
- Self talk are words
- Auto suggestions are words

Trash Words & Garbage words:

If you fill a trash can up with trash, you will not have any clean space in your trash can. If you leave the trash in the trash can long enough the trash will begin to rotten and stink. Then you will have a bunch of stinking, rotten garbage on the inside of your trash can.

You have a:

- Trash can in your soul.
- Trash can in your spirit.
- Trash can in your emotions.
- Trash can in your mind.
- Trash can in your physical life.
- Trash can in your finances.

If you allow a lot of trash words to build up in your trash can, you will not have room in your trash can for any positive life giving words. If you allow these trash words to remain inside your trash cans, these trash words will begin to rotten and stink and turn into a:

- Stinking rotten soul.
- Stinking rotten spirit.
- Garbage words in your soul.
- Garbage words in your spirit.

SUCCESS WORDS FOR SUCCESS

- Stinking rotten emotions.
- Stinking rotten mentality.
- Stinking rotten physical environment.
- Stinking rotten financial state.

- Garbage words in your emotion.
- Garbage words in your mind.
- Garbage words in your physicality.
- Garbage words in your finances.

Then life is going to look like a bunch of garbage words to you. Your life is going to look like a bunch of garbage words.

You're going to look life garbage words, act like garbage words, feel like garbage words, and smell like garbage words.

What type of words are considered trash words.

The following are some trash words:

Pessimistic words	Failure words	Profanity Words
Negative words	Fear words	Poverty Words
Dead words	Racist words	Lack words
Hateful words	Prejudice words	Mad words
Hurtful words	Defeat words	Depressed words

To get rid of these words do and say the following:

I am that I am is a part of the universal power expressed in the physical form. I have the powers of the universe within me.

I am that I am now is cleaning all the trash words and garbage words out of my soul.

I am that I am now is cleaning all the trash words and garbage words out of my spirit.

I am that I am now is cleaning all the trash words and garbage words out of my emotions.

I am that I am now is cleaning all the trash words and garbage words out of my mind.

I am that I am now is cleaning all the trash words and garbage words out of my physical environment.

I am that I am now is cleaning all the trash words and garbage words out of my finances.

I am that I am now is cleaning all the trash words and garbage words out of my situations.

I am that I am now is cleaning all the trash words and garbage words out of my opportunities.

I am that I am now is cleaning all the trash words and garbage words out of the inside of me.

I am that I am now is cleaning all the trash words and garbage words out of my words:

CHAPTER 3

YOUR WORDS ARE YOU

Words impact our:

Soul	Confidence	Self image	Achievement
Spirit	Success	Self esteem	Personality
Emotions	Prosperity	Love	Character
Mentality	Money	Happiness	Disposition
Physically	Feelings	Energy	Career

Words are with you all of your life. You should make your words work for you, not against you.

Listen and learn

There is a saying. A person that kept their mouth shut kept their soul. That means if a person does not open their mouth to speak you will not be able to adequately assess, analyze & determine their character.

Once a person begins to speak, listen to their choice of words.

People's choice of words will differ because they have had a different: upbringing, cultures, experiences, environments & education.

Content

What words do they use?
What subject do they speak about?
What words do they use quite often?

PERSON A

- Please sit down
- Go back and get it
- I got your back
- Last night
- They make me sick
- He is a pain in the butt
- Go down stairs
- I'm down with you
- What time did you get back

PERSON B

- They are nice
- I trust them
- She is an angel
- Nice guy
- They are fair
- He is honest
- She has a good heart
- I love that smell

PERSON C

- She's Jealous
- He is hating that
- They're envious
- They're a player hater
- They don't like me
- She's a flirt
- He is a thief
- He lies a lot
- You can't trust them
- They will hurt you.

PERSON A CHOICE OF WORDS:

- Back
- Down
- Last
- Sick
- Def
- Pain

PERSON B KEY CHOICE OF WORDS:

- Nice
- Trust
- Angel
- Fair
- Honest
- Good

PERSON C CHOICE OF WORDS:

- Problem
- Thief
- Hate
- Lie
- Slick
- Dishonest
- Assault
- Fight
- Jealous
- Hate
- Envious
- Can't
- Flirt
- Thief
- Lie
- Can't
- Hurt

In the Holy Bible we are told:

Your words will become flesh and dwell amongst you as living entities.

Guard your thoughts with all diligence, because out of your thoughts are the issues of lie.

SUCCESS WORDS FOR SUCCESS

May the words of your lips and the meditation of your heart, be acceptable in thy site, oh Lord, My God.

- Words have content. What the word is expressing.
- Heart is your subconscious.
- Words on my lips is the conscious words you use and are conscious of.
- Issues of life are…your experiences from your thoughts and words taking physical form.

Guard your thoughts means you have to monitor the word you:

- Think & use.
- You're around.
- You read.
- You listen to.
- You converse about.

Your words become flesh and dwell amongst you as living things mean:

- What you say you materialize.
- What you say you experience.
- What you say you become.
- What you say you attract to you.

Meditation of your heart is: to repeat, continue to use, or repetitious with a certain word.

When you meditate you are totally engaged in the thought of what you are focused on.

CHAPTER 4

PROGRAM YOURSELF WITH SUCCESS WORDS

SUCCESS WORDS FOR SUCCESS

Meditate on success words & Program your:

- Soul
- Spirit
- Emotions
- Mentality
- Physical
- Finances

Your soul comes from God. Your soul is the life force attributing to you being alive. Words are how you communion with God and your soul. Therefore we can maintain that your soul gives life to your words.

Being that your soul gives life to words, your words are giving you the life you have.

The holy bible says, "May the words of your lips and the meditation of your heart be acceptable in His God's sight."

That is powerful.

Let me elaborate so you understand.

May the words on your lips:

Lip mean:

Thoughts
Consciousness
Tongue
Mind
Surroundings
Prayers
Feelings
Speech
Conversations

Your tongue is part of your conscious mind. You are aware of the words you are using. The words you use are being transported to your: subconscious mind, soul, spirit, emotions, mind, physical body, and finances. Which in turn activates a life force and you experience the word or words in your internal world as a non tangible response in your external world or after world or as a tangible physical response.

May the words of my lips, (speech, thoughts, conversation, or tongue) your conscious mind and the meditation of your heart as in:

- Meditation means to focus
- Meditation means to visualize, to dream.
- Meditation means to imagine, to picture.
- Meditation means repetition, consistent, continued.

The heart is your:

- Soul
- Subconscious mind
- Spirit

Be acceptable in thy site. Be acceptable unto God. Acceptable in society. Acceptable to your confidence, self esteem, positive self image. Acceptable to: providing you the attributes needed to achieve and have the life you're working to have.

May the words on your lips:

- Lips = Thoughts   Speech
         Conscious mind   Conversation

And the meditation:

- Meditation = Visualize   Imagine   Repeating
                Prayer   Picture   Programing
                Focus   Consistency

Of my heart:

- Heart = Subconscious mind

Be acceptable in thy site

- Thy site = God
  Soul

Even the bible says let the weak say I am strong.

If you make a remark you did not mean, and in front of, use it enough, it will stick and be programmed within you then experienced on the outside of you and inside of you.

Internally and externally.

Internally as:

Love	Joy	Motivation
Charisma	Peace	Inspiration
Happiness	Confidence	Tranquility
Self esteem	Forgiveness	Contentment
Optimism	Positive Self image	

Externally as:

Money	Spouse	Yacht
College Degree	Lier Jet	Home
Promotion	Olympic Medal	Spouse
Health	Car	Family
Job	Relationship	Children
Career	Success	Prosperity

If you continually use a remark or a phrase you will experience what you say.

Remarks like:

- If you didn't have bad luck, you wouldn't have any luck.
- You're a pain in the butt.
- You make me sick and tired.
- The economy is bad.
- Poor little children.
- Poor thing.
- Sick and tired of you.
- They make me sick.

Phrases on tattoos like:

- Born to lose.
- Death.
- Bad luck.
- Cursed.
- Dirty.
- Suicide.
- Homicide.
- Killer.

Nick names like:

- Dumbo
- Lower
- Funk
- Clown
- Hobo
- Bumey
- Broke
- Tired

SUCCESS WORDS FOR SUCCESS

Your words program your:

Soul	Career	Money
Spirit	Confidence	Family
Emotions	Self esteem	Opportunities
Mind	Self image	Situations
Physical	Achievement	Experiences
Finances	Accomplishments	Charisma
Social life	Marriage	Friends
Spouse	Relationships	Success
Children	Job	

Your words program your life.

Good news is you can start now to create the new you and the new life you want.

By changing the words of what you have, to using the words of what you want.

CHAPTER 5

THE MAGIC OF WORDS

SUCCESS WORDS FOR SUCCESS

If you don't take the time to use the right success words, you won't take the time to do the right success work.

If you take the time to use the right success words you will take the time to do the right success work to get the right success results. That is how you get magic out of words.

What is magic and what are words?

Magic is when you do and say something a certain way for a wanted result.

Words are what you use to describe everything in existence.

There are two types of magic. Magic for entertainment as with a magician that does tricks like pulling a rabbit out of hats.

Then there is magic you use for real life.

- Magic to physically materialize thousands of dollars, millions of dollars, or billions of dollars.

This chapter is about words of magic for you obtaining the life you want.

You might ask show difficult will it be? And how long will it take?

How is the easy part? The only difficulty you will encounter is you. Everything else is waiting for your command.

How long will it take, 1 second? It will happen in the twinkling of an eye.

- Words are magic
- Words have power

- Words heal
- Words create

Magic words are you using and only using the words of what you want, in your life.

CHAPTER 6

I AM THE WORDS I SAY

SUCCESS WORDS FOR SUCCESS

In the Bible, words are used to bring light from darkness. God said, "Let there be light"

When we think we use words to describe our thoughts.

If we are thinking positive thoughts we use positive words. If we are having negative thoughts, we use negative words.

The words we use are programming our subconscious mind through our conscious mind.

A wise man once said a man that keepeth his mouth, keepeth his soul. What that is saying is until a person talks to you, you are not able to obtain information about them. However once they begin to talk and use words, you will begin to form certain impression about them that are beyond their physical appearance, ethnicity, car, home, education, money, & social status.

The words we say, words we think, influence how we feel and influences how much we accomplish.

The great part about words is they affect you for the good if you want them to.

However, they can affect you for the bad even if you do not want them to.

You have to be the Gate keeper of the words you allow yourself to:

- Be around
- Listen to
- Read

The Bible tells us to guard our heart with due diligence because out of them come the issues of life.

Your heart is:

- Your soul
- Your spirit
- Your conscious mind
- Your subconscious mind

The Bible clearly states your words will become flesh and dwell amongst you as living entities.

Your words can be your:

- Thoughts
- Feelings
- Mentality
- That which you visualize
- That which you imagine.

The issues in life as in guard your heart with due diligence because out of the heart comes the issues of life, meaning:

- What you experience
- Your circumstance
- Your situations

Are all correlated to words.

CHAPTER 7

GOD IS MY WORDS

MY WORDS ARE GOD

Control your words, or they will control you.

If a word attempts to hijack you simply say no. That word is not me after not.

If a word is in your mind, your spirit, and your emotions, your physical environment, that you do not want, tell yourself that word is not me.

Tell the word, that is not me. This is the word I am. Then say the word, that you are.

Let's look at some examples:

- Hate is a word.

Tell yourself this word is not me. I am love.

What type of words would you use if you were best friends with God? And be with God every day. News alert. You are with God every day.

God is with you according to the level of words you allow yourself to be preoccupied with that identify with who and what God is. If you use words, feel words, think words or your physical environment and actions are words contrary to God. The opposite of what God is then that will lessen the presence of God with in you.

CHAPTER 8

COMMAND YOUR WORDS

SUCCESS WORDS FOR SUCCESS

Words command:

- How we feel
- What we think
- What we do
- How far we go
- What we accomplish
- How much we get
- What our career is

How is it that words command us?

In order to have an order carried out, you must first give the command.

Hang with God 24 hours a day & 7 days a week. You are best friends with God. The words you use in your thoughts, feelings and conversations should be words that please God, words that God uses.

- What type of words does God use?
- What type of word feelings does God feel?
- What type of word thoughts does God think?
- What type of word pictures does God form?

You are made in the image of God. Your Words should reflect God, Words like:

Forgive	Good	Joy	Supernatural	Winner	Royalty
Fun	Great	Peace	Overflow	Success	Diamonds
Health	Prosperity	Plenty	Silver	Wealth	Infinite
Energy	Gold	Abundance	Humongous	Surplus	
Unity	Big	Possible	Overcome	Perseverance	
Create	Accomplish	Millionaires	Achieve	Yes	
Patience	Love	Billionaires	Champion	Provide	

In order to have an order carried out, you must first give the command.

- FIRST, we soulfully give life to words.

- SECOND, we spiritually embrace a word, giving the word energy.

- THIRD, we mentally think of the word and the definition of the word, then create a picture of the word.

- FOURTH, we emotionally respond to the word through feelings

- FIFTH, we physically act on the word through our ACTIONS

Based on our actions we have made a:

Choice and decision.

You can have a thousand words however the word that you make a decision on gives power to the word. We are told in the Bible Genesis that God used words to begin the process of life as we know it.

God created through words.

God's creation of the universe was orchestrated through thought that had to be administered through the power of words in that each word commanded a certain instruction, direction, cause and effect.

In God gave his choices and decisions a word that were used to describe his thoughts, emotions, spirit, vision and directives.

God used words to create.

Since you were born, you have been surrounded with words.

Words from your:

- Parents
- Doctors
- TV
- Radio
- Books
- Advertisements
- School
- People
- Internet

On a daily basis you are bombarded constantly with thousands of words. You think thousands of words. You feel thousands of words. However you do not act on those thousands of words unless you allow these words to be programed in your soul, spirit, emotions, mind and subconscious mind. This is accomplished through and from repetition.

There are studies that suggest you can hear and read something 1 time to be programmed. To deprogram what took you 1 time to hear, see or read, will take you 5 to 10 times hearing, seeing or reading the opposite to change it.

That is one of the reasons certain good or bad habits are challenging to change.

Good habits:

Punctuality
Forgiveness
Smiling
Loving
Caring
Disciplined
Cleanness
Well kept
Giver

Bad habits:

Promiscuity
Hate
Anger
Drugs
Alcohol
Gambling
Pornography
Unkept
Untidy
Stingy

CHAPTER 9

MY WORDS ARE MY LIFE

SUCCESS WORDS FOR SUCCESS

Words have life, spirits and energy to them. You must decide what words on a daily basis you will allow yourself to:

- Have In your spirit
- Think
- Feel
- Contemplate
- Visualize
- Imagine
- Identity with
- Say
- Speak
- Listen to
- Read
- Words that another person or a lot of people use
- Listen to through music
- Be around that other people use
- Identify with

One sure way to start your day off, during your day and when you go to sleep at night time is to give yourself verbal commands through prayer.

Delete certain words out your life, reprogram your soul, spirit, body, emotions and mind to be words you want to live.

You determine the word you are not.

Choose you this day which words will serve you.

- You are the words that you use. Your words program you.

- Your emotions are programmed by your words.

- Your subconscious mind is programmed by your words.

- Your physical body is programmed by words.

- Your money, achievements, success and prosperity is programmed by your words.

The great news is now you know. The words you hear, words you read, words of the people you are around, words you think a lot about, words you see a lot, and the words you allow yourself to feel a lot, effect you.

If you do not like the experience of a word you use, stop using the word. How do you know which words you should not use?

Ask yourself this, do you want the result of the word you are using?

Words like:

- Hate:

    I hate a rainy day instead of using hate you would say. I prefer a beautiful and sunny day. Using the word hate a lot would program hate inside your soul spirit, emotions and mind.

- They make me sick and tired: Saying this with attribute to the person saying this becoming sick and tired.

CHAPTER 10

MAGIC ATOMIC WORDS

Word Magic.

Magic is when you make something happen out the ordinary. As in to make it happen because you said it would.

To make it happen against the odds. To make it happen quicker than it was supposed to.

We all have our own ideal about what magic is. One thing we all can agree on about magic, is this; make magic happen someone has to do something.

Someone has to say:

> Watch me do this by doing this. Watch me make this happen by saying this. And when you make it happen, people will consider that magic.

I'm saying watch the magic you make happen by:

- Using magic atomic words.

- Thinking magic atomic words.

- Feeling magic atomic words.

- Emotional intensity of magic atomic words you say.

- Focusing on magic atomic words.

- Repetition of magic atomic words.

- Listening to magic atomic words.

- Writing magic atomic words.

- Reading magic atomic words.

- Being around people who use magic atomic words.

- Music with magic atomic words.

- Prayers with magic atomic words.

- Signing magic atomic words.

- Being around magic atomic words.

- Clothing with magic atomic words on them.

- Having a tattoo with magic atomic words.

Magic, is no different than taking off weight. In order to reach a desired weight you have to be disciplined and program yourself to take the weight off. Yes, this will require a fight on your part.

You have been programmed to use, think, feel, act and be certain words. Those words feel they can invade your soul, spirit, emotions, mind and physical behavior anytime they want.

You have to make a stand and fight the old you for the new you in order for your magic to happen.

When a word attempts to be you and that is not you, tell yourself that word that I'm feeling, thinking, doing and being is not me. Then say the word you are. Tell yourself, this is the word I am.

I know a man that used to say one of his children were a pain in the butt.

Guess what he developed, a nagging pain in his tail bone, his butt.

If can have adverse effects on you, then words can have positive effects on you.

You have to be alert as to the words you are retaining. Let's take a short survey of the words in your:

SUCCESS WORDS FOR SUCCESS

- Atmosphere = What words describe your atmosphere; in your environment?

- Soul = What words have you given life to?

- Spirit = What words do you feel?

- Emotions = What words describe how you respond?

- Mind = What words do you think and visualize?

- Physical = What words describe your behavior. Your actions?

- Environment = What words describe where you live Your home, your neighborhood?

Now let's use memory words

- Past= What words do you identify your past with?

    What words do you use to describe your past?

- Present= What words do you describe your present with?

    What words do you use in your present?

- Future= What words do you see, hear, feel & contemplate about your future?

You can change how you feel about your past, present & future by changing your word choice.

If you do not like the results you are getting in life, change the words you are using to the words that describe the results you want. If you do not take the time to use the word of the result you want, you will not take the time to do the necessary work to get the results you want.

If you take the time to use the words of the results you want you will take the time needed, to do the necessary work to get the results you want.

You are the words you chose to say. Your repetition of certain words has attributed to you being who you are.

Listen to the words your doctor, politician, lawyers, clergy, psychologist, psychiatrist, banker and law enforcement use. They use words of what & who they are.

Listen to the words star athletes use. Listen to the words achievers, winners and champions use. They use the words of what and who they are.

Listen to the words millionaires, multi millionaires, billionaires and multi billionaires use. They use the words of what and who they are.

Listen to the words confident vs. incompetent people use.

Listen to the words of people who are poor, live in poverty areas and are underachievers.

Listen to the words of people who are rich, live in prosperous areas and are achievers.

The words they use are the indicator of their soul and spirit. The words they use tell you who and what they are.

I have observed how many people do not want to let their anti success, counterproductive words go.

Even though you point out to them how certain words are not good for them, succeeding, winning, and prospering. They keep saying those same anti success, counterproductive words. Words like:

Back, down, last, can't, hate, behind, stupid, dumb, pain, poor, little, lack, not enough, worse, bad, lost, impossible, and many more self defeating words.

I have observed that people who use these words often are miserable, poor, confrontational, mad, pessimistic, angry & argumentative.

When you are around a person long enough, they have a tendency to rub off on you, in that you slightly become some of who they are. How do you know what and who you are with? Listen to the words they use and the content of their verbal or written communication with you.

If they always use truth, trustworthy and honest when they are talking about another person or subject then it is most likely they are trust worthy, tell the truth and are an honest person. This is not an exact science so make sure their actions and behaviors coincide with their words.

Yes my friend actions do speak louder than words. However words will tip you off, about who you are dealing with.

Their words will tell you what they did to or for another person. And you are probably next in line. Because if they did it to them then they will or could do it to you. Be it bad or good, negative or positive.

When you are around a person you can program them to picture and visualize whatever picture of you, you want them to see you as. When they are preparing to go to sleep at night, they will, see your face, then hear the content of the words you used when they were around you.

Words like:

- You look very nice.

- What and a billion dollar smile.

- Great to see you.

- Hello Mr. Campion.

- Hello Mrs. Winner.

- I love this day.

- The world is a better place because you are here.

- You are blessed and highly favored.

- You are 1 special person.

- When I grow up I want to be like you.

- Hello Mrs. Millionaire.

Make sure you are truthful with your compliments.

Whenever you talk to another person, somehow use words with positive magic atomic energy: Words like:

Yes	Prosper	Overcome	Trust	Millionaire
Plenty	Forgive	New	Forgive	Like
Surplus	Achieved	Happy	Family	Accept
Trust	Winner	Peaceful	Unity	Include
Love	Courage	Joy	Billions	Nice
Won	Great	Love	Opportunity	Loyal
Can	First	Loyalty	Healthy	Well
Possible	Power	Top	Forward	Success
Prosperity	Improved	Bright	Sunny	Surplus

Write your own list of the atomic magic words that describes you.

I want you to get a blank piece of paper. Then you will need a couple of pens, or a couple of pencils. You will need a time clock or regular watch and set it for 10 minutes. Anything you write after 10 minutes will not count.

SUCCESS WORDS FOR SUCCESS

This is a once in a life time offer. You have exactly 10 minutes to fill in the atomic words of who you are, what you are, how you want to feel, and what you want to accomplish.

Here are some examples:

Go to heaven	Love	Spouse
Forgive	Health	Children
Be forgiven	Happiness	Youthful energy
Forgive myself	Energy	I forgive myself
God forgive me	Youthfulness	Lier Jet
God forgive them	Success	3 mansions
They forgive me	Prosperity	Rolls Royce
Wealth	Power	A wife
Friends		A husband

Make 100 billion dollars so I can personally have 10 billion in the bank.

So I can give family members 100 million dollars.

Have my corporate buildings and 1,000 employees.

Win the Nobel Peace Prize in the field of self help.

Be the keynote speaker at The White House.

Sell 100 million books.
Sell 100 million CD's.
Sell 100 million DVD's.

Win a Diamond Award.
Win 10 Pulitzers prizes.
Win 10 Grammy awards.

Be a Unites States Senator.

- Prosperity
- Wealth
- Love
- Joy
- Peace
- Drug free
- Alcohol free
- Tobacco Free

Have my own TV station.
Have my own radio station.

My wife, mother, step father, children, grandchildren, brothers, sisters, nieces and nephews all come together and make peace. Have unconditional love between us. Have a healthy, wealthy, successful and prosperous life with each other.

I will have mansions in California, Florida, New Jersey, Paris.

- Have a large Yacht with a staff of 25.

- Have a large leer jet that can fly 30 people at the same time.

- Have my own train for me and family.

- Have my own helicopters.

- Have corporate buildings for Right Choice Success Corporation and be world wide with 1 billion consumers of our success products.

Live to be 109, wife live to be 110 and all my children live to be 112.

Be able to improve the lives of people on planet Earth and make planet Earth a better place to live on.

Nine minutes have passed, I have 1 minute left.

What will my final magic atomic word be?

That you have the life you write on your magic atomic word list.

Now you have given yourself 10 minutes and wrote your atomic words on a piece of paper.

- Who you are
- What you are
- What have you accomplished
- What you want
- How much you want

After 10 minutes put the pen and pencil up, now read your magic atomic words about yourself.

Your magic atomic word list you make is true. The magic atomic word list you make is you.

My first magic atomic words were saved so you will remember them. To ask God for His favor and a double anointing, so I can better and effectively serve His creation. Human beings. That God will lead and direct me in all that I do. And that God always finds me worthy to serve you.

CHAPTER 11

19TH POWER WORDS

Since you have written your atomic word list, these are the words you are living.

If the words you are around or words that are around you through your: ears, vision and someone's mouth, are not what you want in your life then remove yourself from them or remove them from you.

Because of the counterproductive words you hear and see each day.

I have created a subliminal, self hypothesis, auto suggestion atomic word program called 19th power.

The 19 Power book is a scientific program created by Dr. AJ Rolls.

19th Power program counteracts the subliminal and auto suggestive words you have been programmed with, without your permission. 19th Power will counteract what has been done to you.

Enjoy the most you can of this life. You are special to people when you die, however you are special to me while you are alive.

Here are some common everyday words that will bring atomic word power to you and provide a magic response from people.

Words like.

1. It was my fault.
2. Please forgive me.
3. I am sorry.
4. You are appreciated.
5. I love you.
6. I appreciate you.
7. You're valuable to me.

8. I made a mistake.

9. Are you okay.

10. I did not intend to hurt you.

11. I need you.

- Words can heal a person in sorrow.

- Words can comfort a lonely person.

- Words can encourage a person that is discouraged.

- Words can make happy a person that is sad.

- Words are healing agents when used correctly.

- Words can build a person that has been torn down.

The Magic of words. Whatever you experience, a word has been assigned to it by a person.

Words have been assigned to you by a person to describe you.
The way you treat another person, a word has been assigned to it.
The way you talk to another person, a word has been assigned to it.

You can work magic when you know how to work with the words of how you want to be perceived, remembered, described, and considered to be.

Think about a person you know.

You have most likely assigned words to describe them.

Once you think about them the words you have assigned to them will become alive in that those words will affect you first mentally, then emotionally.

SUCCESS WORDS FOR SUCCESS

You have used words to describe the person.

You will feel the experience of remembering the people use words to describe them self.

Certain people use words to describe them self.

- Multi billionaires use certain words.

- Millionaires use certain words.

- Politicians use certain words.

- Winner use certain words.

- Losers use certain words.

- Under achievers use certain words.

- Quitters use certain words.

As you see certain people, use certain words consistently and repetitively.

What group of people will you place with the following word choices I use in a sentence?

- I want to but it will probably be too hard to achieve. What type of person says this? What word describes them?

- We will achieve this plan if we all work together with cooperation from each other.

- There is plenty of everything on planet Earth for everyone.

- I believe in you.

- You are stupid and retarded.

- I could get ahead in life if it weren't for all the discrimination.

- Today is just another day.

- There is more money for me.

- I believe we can do what other people say cannot be done.

As you see words have a life of their own. Once a word is released it has an atomic ripple effect.

Strive to be an artist of words. Paint or draw pictures with your words. Life is your canvas.

The Magic of Words can and do provide magic every day.

CHAPTER 12

PAINT A PICTURE WITH YOUR WORDS

When you tell someone you love them and really do love them, this provides healing to their soul, spirit, emotions, mind and body.

If you really want to influence a person in a positive way use words to give them an honest compliment.

Use atomic words when texting, emailing, writing and speaking, but most of all in communication with yourself. Words like:

You, we, us, our, family, love, team, united, unity, together, loyalty, truth, honest, plenty, authentic, special, dependable, needed, God, Jesus, happy, joy, peace, tranquility, share, earnest, like, enjoy, optimistic, energy, sun, spring, up, positive, prosper, success, winner, achiever, good, great, accomplish, millionaire, billionaire, abundance, forgive, possible, can, ours, include, won, champion, up, first, victory, family, change, improve, right, agree, first and yes.

You will communicate pleasure to them. Your words will communicate directly with their subconscious level on a subliminal level in that they will enjoy you, like you, and remember you in a good way because you subliminally communicated with their subconscious mind.

There is nothing bad about this in that when people like you magic happens for the both of you.

People may not like your color, or your ethnicity however because you have appealed to their sub conscious mind and subliminally connected with their positive side, they accept and like you.

Words have a soul and spirit. Soul as in they have life. Spirit as in they have energy that attaches themselves to people. Words are the language of your soul. Words have an effect on people. Be the person that knows how to paint a beautiful picture with words.

Have you noticed how beautiful greeting cards are however the real beauty and gem is the words chosen to express an emotion?

When you write a resume for a potential employer, your words establish a soul life first, then spiritual energy. This spiritual energy will elicit an emotion. This emotion will attribute to their mind developing the emotion into a picture. Your resume on a metaphysical level will transport positive energy, all because of the words you use to describe yourself and your employment history.

I could have wrote this book Success Words with just one page. By saying use the words of the results you want.

Think about a new born baby. Think about the words people have internalized when thinking about a baby. Look at the words used to paint a picture of a baby.

1. Innocent
2. New
3. Harmless
4. Pure
5. Devine
6. Miracle
7. Honest
8. Trust Worthy
9. Non judgmental
10. Accepted
11. Loving
12. Special
13. Authentic
14. Hold
15. Cuddle
16. Embrace
17. No threat
18. Safe
19. Love
20. Clean
21. Cute
22. Trust

If people identify you with these words listed, how do you think everybody would feel about you, think about you, remember you as.

Just about everybody likes and loves a baby.

Case and point.

Attempt to embrace some of the words associated with being a baby. No matter how old you are you can still adopt some powerful word choices like:

Trust, authentic, love, God, acceptance, harmless & safe.

Each day attempt to live a new positive word. If each day is too much, live a new word each week. Your words should be words that will help you to better yourself and to help you contribute to the well being of planet Earth.

If every person living on planet Earth at this moment would choose a positive, uplifting, encouraging, loving, forgiving, and empowering word to live each week, how would planet Earth be? Better?

LIVE YOUR WORDS!

What is live your words?

When you live your words you write on a piece of paper what words you are then you live up to the words you've chosen. It's that simple.

Either you choose the words of who you are, or:

- The media will tell you what words you are.
- TV will tell you what words you are.
- Experiences will tell you what words you are.
- Your child hood will tell you what words you are.
- Your ethnicity will tell you what words you are.
- Where you live will tell you what words you are.

- Your programmed emotions will tell you what words you are.

- Your childhood friends will tell you what words you are.

- Racism, discrimination, prejudice and hatred will tell you what words you are.

Choose you right now what words you are and will live as.

Once you choose the words of:

- What you are = A child of GOD.

- Who you are = Special.

- How you feel = Great.

- How you respond = Appropriately.

- How you act = Good manners.

- How you see yourself = Honest.

- What you think of yourself = Winner.

- What you have = Success.

- How much you have = Abundance.

If you act, behave, or respond contrary to how you want to respond, tell yourself that is not me then respond with the word of how you are.

If you respond with the word anger and hostility, tell yourself. This is not the words of who I am. I am these words, calm and friendly, tactful and diplomatic.

SUCCESS WORDS FOR SUCCESS

If you act like the words gullible and afraid tell yourself the words gullible and afraid is not who I am, I am these words assertive and courageous.

- What words do I feel today, right now?
- What words am I thinking right now?
- What words do I want to act out?
- What words do I want to convey today?
- What words are in my soul, spirit, emotions and mind today?
- What word am I visualizing for my life now?
- What words do I want to act like now?

If the words you have chosen are not what you want then do this.

Use the words of what you want and who you are.

God is giving you a choice of the words you are.

CHAPTER 13

I AM THAT I AM ARE THE WORDS I USE

SUCCESS WORDS FOR SUCCESS

You can help other people to see themselves through the words you speak to them, words like:

- You are a really smart person
- It's always great to see you
- Hello Governor
- Hello Money
- Mrs. Achiever
- Mrs. Art student

- Yes
- Sure
- I agree
- You have it
- Very Wise

Be authentic in what you say in your conversation.

- I want to be like you when I grow up
- The world is a better place because you exist in it.

People respond to words. When people lay in their bed at night and go over their time with you, the words you use will impact an emotion about you just from the words you used.

They may not remember what you were talking about but your atomic words will leave a soulful, spiritual, emotional and mental effect on them.

Their words will tell you a lot about what is going on with them. For they will leave a soulful, spiritual, mental and emotional effect on you.

To have a positive impression with a person so use positive words.

You can program a person about you by the word choices you use around them.

To qualify this technique, listen to the words and word sentence of another person.

This will tell you something about the person you are dealing with, and leave an impression about them with you.

Remember, you are one of many people that may use this technique. And it can be used on you. When in doubt look at their behavior, their actions.

An old but true saying is, what you are speaks so loud I do not need to hear what you're saying. Be alert to their words & actions.

Another old saying about words is:

A man or woman that keeps his or her mouth shut, keeps his or her soul.

That means your words tell people what words you have given life to. Your words are your life.

You read a person's soul through their words.

A person can tell a lot about you by your words. The words you identify with are the words that identify you.

Sentences and words like:

- You are great
- Great to see you
- You did a great job
- You're an achiever
- Hello Governor
- Hello Millionaire
- Hello Billionaire
- Mr. Creative
- Ms. Truthful
- You are blessed & highly favored.
- People respond to words.
- God responds to your word choices.
- Your soul responds to words.
- Money responds to words.
- Your spirit responds to words.
- Emotions respond to words.
- Your mind responds to words

Speak the word and get the miracle.

In order to receive a miracle you must use a certain formula of words. Words that activate your soul, and spiritual energy. Words that excite an emotional charge. Words that assimilate and develop a picture using your mind and words that empower your physical body to achieve the physical task at hand.

In order for your body to move, your body requires certain words that command a certain action.

And God said let there be light and there was light. God created the universe as we know it using words.

If you want to create in your own life, to you must use magic atomic words to do so.

You know a person by the company they keep and you know a person by the words they use.

CHAPTER 14

I KNOW YOU BY THE WORDS YOU SAY

Birds of a feather flock together. Words of a kind stick together because words of a person stick with them.

Now that you are more conscious about your words, I have accomplished my objective.

To help you help yourself through:

- Words you say.
- Words you listen to.
- Words you are around.
- Words you feel.
- Words you think.
- Words you act out.
- Words you allow yourself to be around.

My favorite saying is if you don't want the result, then don't use the word.

If you want the result, use the word.

If you take the time to use the word of what you want you will take the time and effort to get the result you want.

I could have wrote a whole book just by saying that.

However I chose to elaborate on a few more significant things about magic atomic words.

The soul of words. Words have life.
The spirit of words. Words have energy.
The emotions of words. Words have feelings.
The mind of words. Words create pictures.

The physicality of words. Words can move.

Because:

- Words are live.

- Words are energy.

- Words have life.

- Words have spiritual energy.

- Words have an emotion.

- Words have a mental picture.

- Words have a life.

In conclusion you are the creator of your words.

You decide what type of day you will have. Words describe your actions.

Be conscious of your words, their words and the words your around because you become the words you:

Listen to	Say	Hear	Write
Are around	Read	Speak	Sing
Poems	Letters	Lectures	Music
Think	Visualize	Imagine	Picture

Make a commitment now today that you will only use the words that reflect you who are. Yours words are the new you.

If you don't take the time to use the right success words of what you want,

you won't take the time to do
what needs to be done to get
the success results you want.

If you take the time
To use the success
words that describe the
success you want. You will
take the time needed to do
what is needed to be done to get the
success results you want.

CHAPTER 15

13 IS A LUCKY NUMBER

I STOPPED SMOKING CIGARETTES ON THE #13.

You will remember that 13 is a lucky number and I did not have to write 300 pages to get my point across.

You do not have to eat the whole cow to know you are eating beef.

You do not have to eat a whole chicken to know you are eating chicken.

You do not have to eat fish for 7 days to know you are eating fish.

I do not have to write you three hundred pages to articulate to you how important the:

- Words you think are.
- Words you say are.
- Words you listen to are.
- Words you read are.
- Words you look at are.
- Words your around are.
- Words you hear are.
- Words you joke about are.
- Words you say and do not mean are.
- Words you represent as are.

The objective of this book is to be short and to the point.

I want you to remember, benefit from and receive wanted results from what you have learned more, then for you to be impressed with the large amount of pages written to get my point across.

The modest amount of pages provided to you in this book I pray will be life changing for you and the other people you share my work with.

This book, "Success Words For Success," objective is to inform you about the power of your words.

To inform you on how to use your words to work for you not against you.

Words for success does not want you to attempt to be flawless, mistake free and have a perfect 24 hours without, error meaning you use an incorrect word, feel a incorrect word, think an incorrect word or your actions and behavior are an incorrect word.

That's why you and I are officially saying goodbye to perfect.

Words for success is about helping you to be aware, not perfect. Help you to apply words in your daily life that are healthy for you.

You are now aware of the atomic power of your words and their effect on:

Your soul	Your money
Your spirit	Your confidence
Your emotions	Your self esteem
Your mind	Your success
Your physical body	Your prosperity
Your marriage	Your energy
Your relationships	Your motivations
Your achievements	Your family

Your words are instrumental in commanding the atoms to assimilate, develop, and form what you say, into materialization tangible success, and intangible success.

Your words are your atomic keys to unlock the atomic power within your prayers.

Just because you sin, by saying incorrect words, repent and forgive yourself. Even the Holy Bible instructs us to forgive 70 x7 each day.

I promise you at this great time of your historic life and yes my friend this is a very special time of your life. You do not want to be perfect. Why?

Perfect people would tell you why if they could. However, their perfect address does not allow them to tell you why. The address for perfect people is:

- Grave yard
- Morgue
- Funeral Home

- Cemetery
- Some hell
- Some heaven

Goodbye perfect.

Have fun with your new knowledge of atomic words.

- Think any word you want.
- Feel any word you want to feel.
- Visualize a word in video from.
- Imagine a word in picture form.
- Picture the words of life you want.
- Listen to the words of other people and use their words will tell you something about them.
- Look at the words of who you are. In your home, your career, your hobbies.

Hence forth my friend enjoy the amazing world of success words.

SUMMARY & CONCLUSION

I AM

I AM my new blessings.
I AM my new changes.
I AM my new soul.
I AM my new spirit.
I AM my new emotions.
I AM my new mind.
I AM my new physical.

Summary

Your words can make you or your words can break you.

Your words will make you who you want to be or your words will make you who you do not want to be.

Words are like a magic gene. We get what we speak.

No matter what your life is like now, if you change your words, you will change your life.

Words are atomic power in that once released there is an immediate ripple effect that will cause a change. Whatever the word is that is the change you receive.

- Think of your soul as a garden. What words have you planted?
- Think of your spirit as a garden. What words have you planted?
- Think of your emotions as a garden. What words have you planted?
- Think of your mind as a garden. What words have you planted?
- Think of your physical as a garden. What words have you planted?
- Think of your money as a garden. What words have you planted?

Your words are the seeds you plant in these gardens.

You cannot plant a watermelon seed in your garden and expect to get bananas.

Whatever type of seed you plant, that is what you will grow. That is what you will harvest.

The Holy Bible reminds us:

As you sow, so shall you reap.
What type of words are you sowing in your life?

What type of words are you sowing when you talk to other people in conversation?

When people think of you what words would they use to describe you?

What words do you identify with and use regularly?

What words do you allow yourself to:

- Think
- Feel
- Meditate on
- Dream
- Be
- Visualize
- Imagine

You have the power to:

Be the words you choose to use.

Once you begin your new life of being the words you choose to be, there will be some resistance from your:

- Soul = life
- Spirit = Energy
- Emotions = feelings
- Mental = pictures and thoughts
- Physical = behaviors and actions

Your soul is your life. Your soul is life. Your soul gives life to your words. There may be some resistance from your very own soul to give life to your new words. How do you defeat this?

Your desire to have the positive change of words will win. Be patient and consistent.

Your spirit is an energy and the energy of the old words may attempt to challenge the energy from the new words however the new words will win. Be aware, and if you use the old words, correct yourself.

Emotions. Emotions are feelings and we get use to certain feelings when certain words are triggered in us attributing to a certain feeling. There will be some resistance there. Be aware and correct yourself if you give the wrong response or feeling.

Mentally our minds paint pictures with the words we use. The old picture may attempt to surface when we speak a word that identifies with a certain picture. You may for a period get the picture you do not want. If this happens be aware and paint the picture of what you want in your mind, by using certain words.

Physically our body carries out the orders it receives from our choice of words. You are use to behaving, actions, and responding a certain way, depending on the words being used to communicate the setting you are in. If the old unwanted response happens, check yourself.

Even though you may have responded in a way you shouldn't, or in a way you do not want to, correct yourself. Tell yourself, the words or word you should have responded as.

The top line my friend is this:

If you use a word you do not want to use anymore, tell yourself that word is not me anymore. Then tell yourself the new word you are.

If you are feeling a word you do not want to feel tell yourself, that word is not how I want to feel. This is the word I feel.

Metaphysically speaking, you have powers above and beyond any gravitational pull of earthly people, places and things, all of which are governed by words. Words created them, and words maintain them.

They are subordinate to your atomic word power you possess within your words.

You have the metaphysical powers to choose the atomic words of how you think, feel and act.

Remember we spoke about you having a garden and your words are the seeds.

As with my garden you have to be alert to weeds. Weed are inevitable.

You have to be alert to weeds and varmint. Weeds and varmints that attempt to take what you have labored to grow in your garden.

The weeds and varmints are symbolic of the old words attempting to take over the new words. Don't allow it.

By telling the old words that is not me anymore, "This is who I am. Now. This is the word I am." Say, think, and feel, your new word.

If a person is too lazy to use the word of who they say they are, they will be too lazy to do the work required to be who they say they are.

If you take the time to use the words or word of who you are, you will take the time to get the result of who and what you are, by taking the time. to do the work to get the result of who you say you are.

NOTE: If a person does not respect God and the name of God, do you really think they respect you. People who cuss by saying, the cuss word GOOD... once a person shows me they do not respect the name of God, I have a special way of dealing with them.

The New Beginning

Success Resurrector
Dr. AJ Rolls, Msc.D., Ph.D., B.s.s.

WORDS

Words make you or break you.
Words help you or hurt you.
Words build or tear down.
Words save or destroy.

You have been programmed by your words. Your words determine what you are, who you are, what you accomplish, what you have and what you do.

Certain words you think, say and use to communicate, it does not matter what you are speaking about you will find a way to integrate those words without your conscious effort. Meaning without you intending to use them. You just spontaneously use them.

The words you think, feel, use, read, listen to and be around will determine:

- What you achieve in your life
- How much money you require
- If you will marry
- Your level of success
- Your level of prosperity
- The car you drive
- The type of home you live in
- How you look
- How you dress
- How you feel
- Who you socialize with
- If you obtain a college degree
- How affluent you are.

The words you use are instructing, directing, assembling, forming and developing your life.

- Learn how to write a picture from your life with your words.
- Say the words and receive the miracle.
- Fix your life by fixing your words.

- What you say you get.
- Say what you want and get what you say.
- Your words are your key to open the doors to:
    - Health, wealth, power, riches, millions, billions, love, companionship, spouse, promotion, achievement, confidence, positive self image, positive self-esteem.

Write/ right your life with your words.

Biography of
Dr. Arthur James Crawford, BSS, Msc.D., Ph.D.
known as

AJ ROLLS
America's #1 Success Resurrector

AJ Rolls (born Arthur James Crawford) has a diploma from the United States Department of Defense in behavioral science, a doctorate in metaphysical science, and a Ph.D. in metaphysical science counseling. He is the founder and chairman of Right Choice Success Corporation and nine subsidiaries. AJ has worked in psychiatry, mental health, social work, and crisis intervention as a behavioral science specialist. He has worked in the New Jersey Maximum Security State Prison as a correction officer, the NJ State Senate, and the NJ State Assembly as a constituent liaison. 2016 he was appointed as Ambassador for the New Jersey 3rd United States Congressional District for the campaign of Congressional Democratic nominee choice. For forty years, he has researched success, prosperity, achievement, personal development, motivation, positive thinking, inspiration, millionaires, billionaires, winners, the subconscious mind, and metaphysical science, focusing on the Science of Success and Success Resurrection.

AJ Rolls has researched failure and success:

- He has acquired education about failure and success.
- He has personally been through numerous failures before he succeeded.
- He has formulated his knowledge of failure and success into a philosophy.
- He has applied this philosophy and achieved the desired result, success.
- He has created the Science of Success Resurrection Philosophy.
- He has created the Success Resurrector.
- He has created the Success as a Way of Life Philosophy.
- He has created the Internal and External Development for Success Philosophy.

- He has created the, Be a Millionaire or Billionaire Now Philosophy.
- He has created the 19th Power Program, which involves subliminal messaging, auto suggestion, and self hypnosis.
- He has authored nineteen Success self help books.
- He has produced and recorded four CD programs.
- He has produced his own movies, "Success Resurrector and 10 * Star OG."
- He has produced a DVD, "Boxing Punches Techniques."

AJ Rolls was mentored by the work of Anthony Norvell who lectured at Carnegie Hall for twenty five years on power of the mind, financial success, and mysteries of the cosmos. Norvell's clientele has included John Paul Getty, Conrad Hilton, Aristotle Onassis, a young Howard Hughes, and Clement Stone.

AJ Rolls' education included the curriculum of Dr. Paul Leon Masters, founder of the University of Sedona and the University of Metaphysics. AJ attended Chapman College, Monterey Peninsula College, Correctional Officer Academy, Behavioral Science School, Rutgers University Entrepreneurial School, Academy of Health Sciences, US Army Missile School, Air Force Community College, Combat Medic School, and Drug and Alcohol School.

As a child, AJ Rolls overcame separation from his parents, along with poverty, welfare, shame, and physical abuse.

As a teenager, he had numerous encounters with gangs, which contributed to him being jumped and severely beaten on four occasions, 3 times guns pulled on him, and being shot. He was stabbed 3 times.

As a young adult, he experienced bankruptcy. He had an addiction to cigarettes, drugs, alcohol, and gambling. He suffered discrimination, legal problems, severe medical conditions, traumatic brain injury, post traumatic stress disorder, being suicidal, and homicidal. He lived in an abandoned home without heat during the winter, and slept on the floor.

AJ Rolls overcame all the obstacles and adversities in his life, which he attributes to God giving him the power to resurrect his life for success, which enables him to help other people resurrect success in their lives as well.

His specialty in the success field is Resurrecting Success spiritually, emotionally, mentally, physically, and financially in the lives of those who have succumbed to misfortune and failure. He coined the phrase <u>SUCCESS RESURRECTOR</u> and created the Science of Success Resurrection Philosophy, formulated into systematic knowledge.

- AJ is a member of the American Metaphysical Doctors Association, and the Prince Hall Fraternity.
- He has been married to his wife, Mary H. Crawford, for thirty three years and has five sons, one daughter and eight grandchildren.
- He is a US Air Force and US Army veteran.
- He is an ordained metaphysical reverend and maintains a close relationship with God.
- He resides in New Jersey.

SUCCESS WORDS FOR SUCCESS

Rightchoicesuccesscorporation.com
(609) 880-1009
259 Nassau Street
PO Box 1224
Princeton, NJ 08542-1224

For further products, go to:

http://www.ajrolls.com
http://www.foundationfornowsuccess.com
http://www.rightchoicesuccess.com
http://rightchoicesuccessinstitute.com
http://www.successpeoplesnetworks.com
http://successpeoplesstore.com
http://19thpower.com
http://successbabeez.com
http://successresearchandprogram/productdevelopmentlaboratories.com

Book AJ Rolls Today for:

- *Lectures*
- *Keynote Speaker*
- *AJ Rolls Tour*
- *Classes*
- *Courses*
- *Personal Appearance*

Books by AJ Rolls:

Open the Safe of Success   *19th Power*
Open the Safe of Winners   *Success Resurrector*
Open the Safe of Thoughts for Success   *Success Help Network.com*
Open the Safe of Affirmations for Success *Success Words for Success*
Positive Revenge or Negative Revenge   *Success Babeez*
Open the Safe of Be a Millionaire Now *Stop Your Excuses*
Open the Safe of Resurrect Success Now *Metaphysical Science for Success*
Be a Millionaire or Billionaire Now   *Success as a Way of Life*
Right Choice Success   *10 * Star OG*
Open the Safe of Purpose, Power & Prosperity

CD's and DVD's by AJ Rolls:

    CD's: *Success Resurrector*
                       19th Power
                       Be a Millionaire or Billionaire Now

    DVD's: *Success Resurrector*
                       Boxing Punches Techniques

19th Power
Success Posters
www.19power.com

TRUST IN GOD

Thank you for buying this success weapon.

Let me know how it has helped you

to help yourself succeed.

Disclaimer

These products are a guide and
individual results will vary depending on
your dedication, consistency
and application as instructed.

CPSIA information can be obtained
at www.ICGtesting.com
Printed in the USA
BVHW081937020519
547214BV00001B/36/P